THIS BOOK
BELONGS TO:

Monrad's

Unlikely Friendships

for Kids

Book Three

The Leopard and the Cow

and Four Other True Stories of Animal Friendships

by

JENNIFER S. HOLLAND

WORKMAN PUBLISHING
NEW YORK

Library of Congress Cataloging-in-Publication Data is available.

ISBN: 978-0-7611-7013-6
Design by Raquel Jaramillo

COVER: © Rohit Vyas; INTERIOR: p. 1, p. 10, pp. 14-15 © Rohit Vyas;
p. 4 Sebastien Burel/Shutterstock; p. 6 Jennifer Hayes; p. 12 Eric
Isselée/Shutterstock; p. 18, p. 22, pp. 24-25, p. 26 © Ron Cohn/Gorilla
Foundation/koko.org; p. 20 Givaga/Shutterstock; p. 28, pp. 32-33 ©
Omer Armoza; p. 31 Liron Pinsover/Dolphin Reef; p. 34 © Houston
Zoo; p. 38, pp. 42-43, p. 44 BARCROFT/FAME.

Workman books are available at special discounts when purchased in
bulk for premiums and sales promotions as well as for fund-raising or
educational use. Special editions or book excerpts can also be created
to specification. For details, contact the Special Sales Director at the
address below, or send an e-mail to specialsales@workman.com.

Workman Publishing Company, Inc.
225 Varick Street
New York, NY 10014-4381

www.workman.com

Printed in the United States of America
First printing April 2012

Contents

Readers new to this series may want to know how I started writing about unlikely animal friendships. Here's the story.

A few years ago, I went scuba diving on Australia's Great Barrier Reef. This is a very special place in the ocean. Thousands of different types of fish live in or around the coral reef.

I noticed a puffer fish swimming near me. The puffer fish was about the size of a softball. He was alone. The puffer fish did not seem to be afraid of me. I swam with him for a little while. He did not swim away.

I went back to the same area the next day. The puffer fish was there. This time, he was

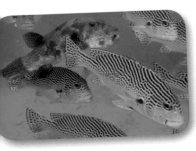 not alone. He was swimming with a school of fish called sweetlips.

Sweetlips are very colorful fish. They have wide mouths, which is probably how they got their name. Sweetlips do not usually swim with puffer fish. But that is exactly what was happening. The sweetlips and the puffer fish were swimming together.

I went back again the next day. They were still together! What was going on? Why were they swimming together? I thought it was very interesting that two animals from different species would be hanging around each other, like they were friends. It made me wonder if other animals became friends with animals that were very different from them.

I am a science writer. I write about animals. So I decided to write a book about animals of different species who had become friends. I had heard some of these stories before. The story of Owen and Mzee, a tortoise and a hippopotamus who became friends after surviving a tsunami, was already famous. But I went looking for stories I had never heard before. I talked with people all around the world. I looked at many photographs. Sometimes the animal friendships were so unlikely that I wondered if they were true. But when I checked them out, they were!

Five of those stories are in this book. I hope you enjoy reading them as much as I enjoyed writing them!

—*Jennifer S. Holland*

Chapter One

The Leopard and the Cow

In India, the cow is considered a sacred animal. It is a symbol of life because it never brings harm to other animals, plus it gives humans the gift of milk. This is why the people of India treat cows with great respect. They don't eat cows. They don't allow anyone to hurt cows.

Early one evening, a young leopard entered a small village in India and began wandering through the streets.

It would be a scary thing to see a leopard walking on your block. Leopards are larger than the biggest of dogs. Their sharp teeth grow to be two inches long. And they are predators.

They hunt and eat many different kinds of prey, including monkeys, reptiles, cows—and humans! So the villagers were right to be very afraid of the leopard.

The villagers did not want the leopard to eat any of their farm animals. When they saw the leopard go into the area where they kept many of their cows, they thought for sure that the leopard was going to eat one.

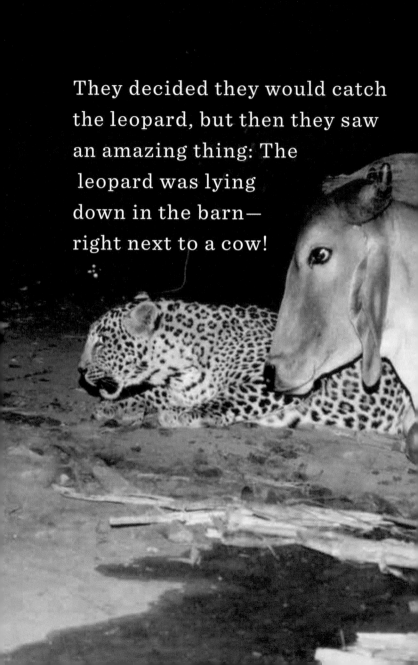

They decided they would catch
the leopard, but then they saw
an amazing thing: The
leopard was lying
down in the barn—
right next to a cow!

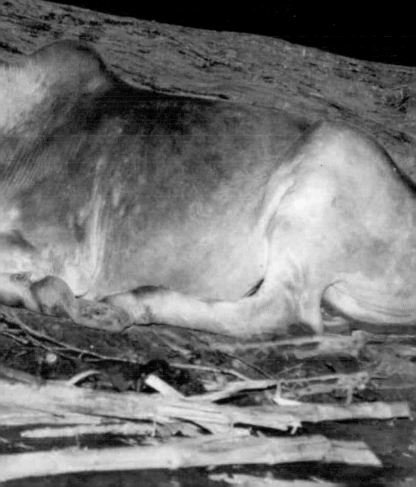

A leopard cuddling with a cow? How could that be? But it was true!

Not only did the leopard
lie down with the cow that
one time; he did it again
and again. For the next sixty
nights, the leopard strolled
into the village, walked
through the streets to the
same place, and lay down
with the same cow.

Sometimes the cow would
lick the leopard from head
to foot. The leopard seemed
to love his tongue bath.
He would close his eyes
in delight.

This sweet little bedtime routine happened every night. Then one day, as suddenly as it had started, it stopped.

No one could explain why the leopard stopped coming. No one had any explanation as to why he had ever started visiting the cow in the first place. All we know is that cows are sacred in India. And friendships—even the most unlikely ones—are sacred everywhere.

Chapter Two

The Gorilla and the Kittens

This is one of the most famous examples of an unlikely animal friendship of all time. It's the story of a sweet gorilla named Koko and three tiny kittens, named All Ball, Lipstick, and Smoky.

Koko, a 230-pound female gorilla who lives in California,

had been taught to communicate using American Sign Language when she was very young. Sign language was invented for people who cannot hear. It is a language made up of hand gestures instead of spoken words. Sometimes the hand gestures tell a story. Sometimes they spell out words. These hands are signing the letters K-O-K-O.

K   O   K   O

Koko's trainer had taught Koko to sign over 1,000 words. One of the words Koko knew how to sign was "cat." This was not surprising. Koko's favorite books were *Puss in Boots* and *The Three Little Kittens*. Koko loved stories about cats. And now, Koko signed that she wanted a cat.

Koko's trainer gave Koko a small stuffed animal kitten. She thought this was what Koko was asking for. But Koko did not want a stuffed animal.

She did not want a toy cat.
Koko wanted a real kitten.

The trainer tried again. This
time she gave Koko a real
kitten for her birthday.
Koko was so happy!

Koko signed her kitten's name as All Ball. Maybe she named her kitten All Ball because he was so tiny that he fit inside the palm of Koko's hand—just like a ball!

Koko was very gentle with All Ball. She signed to her trainer that All Ball was a "soft, good cat." She cuddled All Ball, and let the playful kitten crawl all over her. She didn't mind when All Ball nipped her. She was a very patient friend to the mischievous little kitten.

In time, Koko's trainer gave her two other kittens—Lipstick and Smoky. Lipstick had stripes like a little tiger.

Smoky was a tiny gray kitten
with fur the color of smoke.

Koko loved all her kittens. She
was like a mother to them.

The work Koko's trainer has done with Koko has raised awareness about gorillas, which are an endangered species. There are not many gorillas left in the world. People must work to protect these amazing animals and the habitats in which they live.

Koko has proven that gorillas are not only intelligent, but also capable of the most beautiful of friendships.

Chapter Three

The Dog and the Dolphins

A lot of dogs like the water, but this story is about a dog who liked the animals who live in the water!

Joker was a dog who lived with a family in Israel. Even though he had many human friends, he would sneak away from his family's home to visit

a place called Dolphin Reef
in the Red Sea. This is an area
where marine animals
often interact with humans.
There were other animals
that lived on the land near
Dolphin Reef, too: cats,
chickens—and even some
peacocks.

When Joker first started
hanging around Dolphin
Reef, people thought that he
was there to chase the animals
on land. But Joker was not
interested in those animals.

Joker wanted only to watch
the dolphins! He spent days
watching the dolphins jump
and play in the water.

Then one day, he jumped in to join them! The dolphins did not seem to mind. They all splashed around in the water together.

After a while, Joker's new dolphin friends would whistle and click to him, as if inviting him to join in their games.

Who knows what they were saying to one another? Good friends don't always need words to have a great time together.

Chapter Four

The Zebra and the Gazelle

There is a zoo in Texas where warthogs, zebras, elands, and other animals live together. In the wild, these animals would be living with their own kind. Although none of them is a predator, they sometimes fight over food and access to water. But in the zoo, they all get along.

One day, a young gazelle was brought to live in the zoo. He was very small. The zookeepers worried that he might not be accepted by the rest of the animals— especially the zebras. In the wild, zebras sometimes attack baby gazelles, so the zookeepers kept a very watchful eye on the gazelle and the zebra.

They were surprised by what they saw happen next. One of the female zebras went over to the gazelle. Was she going to attack him? No! She did not attack the young gazelle—she started watching over him! The zebra stayed near him when he rested, and followed him around the zoo. When a warthog started bothering the gazelle, the zebra stood in front of the gazelle and protected him. The zebra even tried to protect the gazelle from the zookeepers.

That's what good friends do, after all: They keep an eye on each other.

Chapter Five

The Rhinoceros and the Warthog

Tatenda was a rhinoceros who was very lucky to be alive. When he was just three months old, poachers killed his entire herd. He was the only survivor. Poachers are hunters who illegally kill animals in order to sell their hides or, in the case of rhinos, their horns. Poaching is one reason that

rhinos are an endangered
species. There are only
about 4,000 of these amazing
animals left in the wild.

When Tatenda was found,
he was brought to live on a
game reserve in Zimbabwe.
He was safe, but he was very
afraid. And he was lonely.

That's when Poggle came to
the rescue. Poggle was a
baby warthog who also lived
on the reserve. Warthogs
are members of the pig

family who live in the wild. Adult warthogs have tusks that curve upward out of their mouths, to protect them from predators. Baby warthogs don't have tusks, so they have trouble defending themselves if they are separated from adult warthogs. That might have been what happened to Poggle, which is why he ended up on the game reserve where he would be safe. Like Tatenda, Poggle was an orphan.

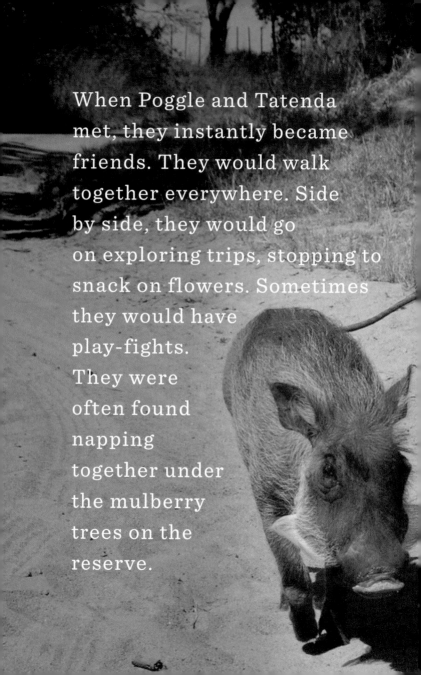

When Poggle and Tatenda met, they instantly became friends. They would walk together everywhere. Side by side, they would go on exploring trips, stopping to snack on flowers. Sometimes they would have play-fights. They were often found napping together under the mulberry trees on the reserve.

The two
buddies
eventually
became
friends
with a third animal: a young
hyena named Tsotsi, who
liked to follow them around
on their adventures.

In time, all three grew big
enough to live in the wild.
Once they were free, would
they still stay together?
At first, they did. But then
Poggle went to live with some

other warthogs. She became a mother of three little warthog piglets of her own. Tsotsi also drifted away— probably to join a clan of hyenas. And Tatenda was accepted by a new herd of rhinos.

We'll never know if the three unlikely friends remembered one another as they grew older, but we do know that they had been there for the others when they were lonely. That's what friends do!

Animal List

 cat: Common house pet that is also an excellent hunter. Cats have been friends with humans for thousands of years. A baby cat is called a *kitten*.

 chicken: Bird that is often raised for its eggs and meat. Chickens make clucking sounds. Many cannot fly.

 cow: Large, four-legged mammal that often lives on a farm and provides humans with milk and meat.

 dog: Common house pet related to the gray wolf. Dogs have been friends with humans for thousands of years.

 dolphin: Small gray whale with a pointed nose and playful behavior. Dolphins live in all the oceans of the world, and even some rivers.

 eland: Four-legged mammal that looks like an ox. Both males and females have twisted horns that point backward.

 gazelle: Four-legged mammal with spiral horns. Gazelles are known for being graceful and fast.

 gorilla: Large African ape that is covered in black hair. Gorillas have no tail, and are much bigger than their chimpanzee cousins.

 hippopotamus: Large mammal that lives in Africa and spends most of the time in the water. Its name means "river horse".

 hyena: Large nocturnal mammal that hunts in packs. Hyenas are known for their call, which sounds like laughter.

leopard: Large cat that lives in southern Asia and Africa. Leopards are known for their light brown coats with many black spots.

 monkey: Small primate that has a furry body and tail. Monkeys live in warm climates, often in tropical forests.

 peacock: Large Asian bird known for its long, bright blue-and-green tail that it can raise behind its head.

 puffer fish: Fish that can puff itself up into a ball and has lots of spines to keep predators away. It is also called a *blowfish*.

 rhinoceros: Large, plant-eating mammal from Africa and Asia that has thick skin and one or two heavy horns on its snout.

 sweetlips: Fish with large lips that often lives in coral reefs. Sweetlips are usually found alone or in small groups.

 tiger: Large cat that lives in Asia and eats other animals. It is known for its orange coat with black stripes.

 tortoise: Reptile that lives on land and is protected by a hard shell. It is closely related to the turtle.

 warthog: Wild African hog with large tusks. Warthogs are named for the two pairs of warty growths on the faces of the males. A baby warthog is called a *piglet*.

 zebra: Four-legged mammal that looks like a horse with black-and-white stripes. Zebras eat plants and are fast runners.

Word and Phrase List

American Sign Language: A language made up of hand positions instead of spoken words; used mainly by deaf people.

clan: A large group of related animals living together.

communicate: To convey information.

coral reef: A chain of underwater coral and limestone rocks near the surface of the ocean where fish and other sea creatures live.

endangered species: A type of animal that may soon become extinct.

game reserve: An area of land where animals live and are visited by tourists.

habitat: The environment where an animal usually lives.

interact: To do things with others.

marine animal: Creature that lives in the sea, like a dolphin or fish.

mischievous: Playful and sometimes a little annoying.

mulberry trees: Plants that grow small purple fruits called mulberries.

orphan: An animal or person whose parents have died.

poacher: A hunter who kills wild animals illegally and then sells their hides, horns, tusks, or other body parts.

predator: An animal that hunts and eats other animals.

prey: An animal that gets hunted and eaten by other animals.

reptile: A cold-blooded animal that usually lays eggs, and has skin covered with scales or bony plates; snakes, lizards, and alligators are all reptiles.

respect: A feeling of admiration for someone or something that is good, valuable, or important.

sacred: Deserving respect or honor.

scuba dive: To swim underwater with an oxygen tank and goggles.

species: A group of animals of the same kind.

survivor: Someone who continues to live after a hardship.

symbol: Something that stands for something else.

tsunami: A big sea wave, caused by an earthquake or a volcanic eruption under the sea, that often leads to a flood.

tusk: Very long tooth that sticks out of an animal's mouth; elephants and warthogs have tusks.

zookeeper: A person who takes care of animals in a zoo.